Gus the Bus

By Debbie Croft

Dan has a big, red bus.

The bus is Gus.

Dan gets on Gus.

Mog the dog runs
to get on Gus.

Mog has a big fan!

Jen the hen gets on Gus.

Jen has a rug.

The rug has dots on it.

Nib the bug has a big tub.

Nib sits in the tub

on the bus!

Gus is in the mud!

Gus can not go!

Mog, Jen and Nib
get off the bus.

Gus the bus is **not**
in the mud!

CHECKING FOR MEANING

1. Which animal got on the bus first? *(Literal)*
2. What did Jen take on the bus with her? *(Literal)*
3. Why couldn't Gus go? *(Inferential)*

EXTENDING VOCABULARY

dots	Find the picture of the rug with lots of *dots*. What is another word that has the same meaning as *dots* and rhymes with *dots*?
bug	Listen to the letters in the word *bug*. If you take away the *b* and put another letter in its place, what new words can you make?
tub	Look at the word *tub*. How many sounds are in this word? Can you use these three sounds to make a new word?

MOVING BEYOND THE TEXT

1. Where do you think the animals might be going on the bus? Why?
2. Have you ever been on a bus? Where did you go and why?
3. What are other ways people can travel from place to place?
4. How does the expression on Gus's face match what is happening in the story?

SPEED SOUNDS

Dd	Jj	Oo	Gg	Uu		
Cc	Bb	Rr	Ee	Ff	Hh	Nn
Mm	Ss	Aa	Pp	Ii	Tt	

PRACTICE WORDS

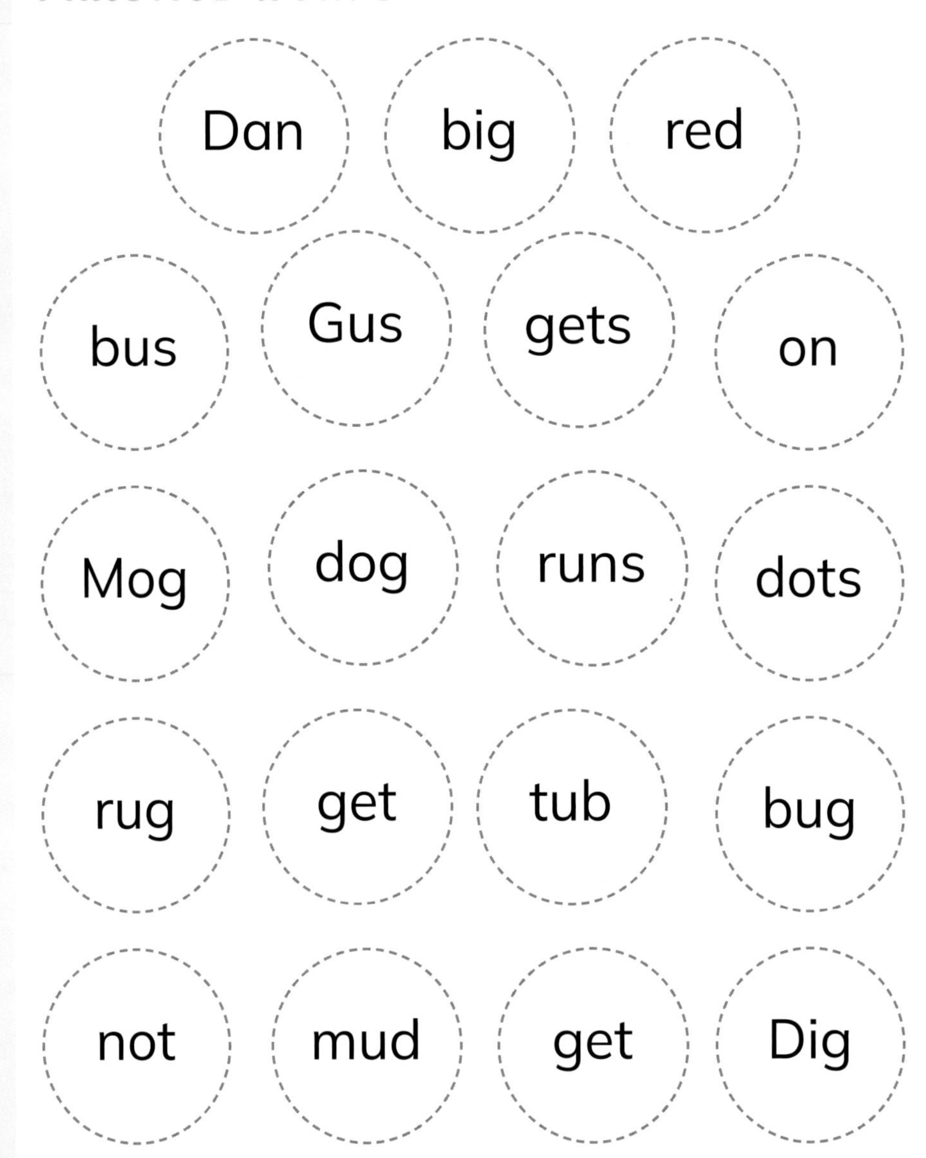